Author:
Anne Rooney lives in Cambridge, England. She studied at Trinity College, Cambridge, where she gained a PhD in an obscure topic and soon after became a full-time writer. She now writes for adults and children, mostly on science and the history of science.

Artist:
David Antram was born in Brighton, England, in 1958. He studied at Eastbourne College of Art and then worked in advertising for fifteen years before becoming a full-time artist. He has illustrated many children's nonfiction books.

Consultant:
Dr Andrew Coburn is Chief Scientist at the Centre for Risk Studies at the University of Cambridge where he carries out research into pandemics, among other risks. Andrew has been an advisor to businesses on their pandemic risk, and was on the UK Government's Scientific Pandemic Influenza Group on Modelling (SPI-M).

Series Creator:
David Salariya was born in Dundee, Scotland. He has illustrated a wide range of books and has created and designed many new series for publishers both in the U.K. and overseas. In 1989, he established The Salariya Book Company. He lives in Brighton, England, with his wife, illustrator Shirley Willis, and their son Jonathan.

Editor: **Nick Pierce**

Published in Great Britain in MMXXI by Book House, an imprint of
The Salariya Book Company Ltd
25 Marlborough Place, Brighton BN1 1UB
www.salariya.com

ISBN: 978-1-913337-77-3

SCRIBO BOOK HOUSE SCRIBBLERS

A CIP catalogue record for this book is available from the British Library.
Printed and bound in China.

Visit
www.salariya.com
for our online catalogue and
free fun stuff.

PAPER FROM
SUSTAINABLE
FORESTS

E-book version available.

You Wouldn't Want to® Be in a Virus Pandemic!

To immunity and beyond!

Written by
Anne Rooney

Illustrated by
David Antram

Created and designed by
David Salariya

A Crisis You'd Rather Not Live Through

BOOK HOUSE
a SALARIYA imprint

Contents

Introduction

Sometimes, you get ill. Usually, after a few days of moping around, you get better and that's it, off you go back to school and to having fun. But sometimes, many people in one area catch the same illness at the same time. That's an epidemic. And occasionally, people in countries around the world fall ill at the same time. That's a pandemic. It can be very disruptive, stopping people doing what they normally do, including going to school, shopping, having holidays and even going to work. It's not good – you wouldn't want to be in a pandemic. But what if you are? Turn the page to find out how to cope!

Every disaster movie starts with a government ignoring a scientist!

You Wouldn't Want to Be in a Virus Pandemic!

What makes you ill?

Your body is usually pretty good at looking after itself if you eat healthy food and take regular exercise, but things can go wrong. Even then, if you've looked after your body, it has a good chance of coping well.

Some illnesses happen because your body doesn't work in quite the right way. People who have diabetes can't control the amount of sugar in their blood, for example. (They can use medicines to help.) You can't catch diabetes from someone else. Other diseases are caused by germs. Many of these can spread between people.

Modern medicine helps us treat or prevent diseases that were once common and deadly, but new diseases emerge. They can cause a pandemic until we develop treatments or vaccines for them.

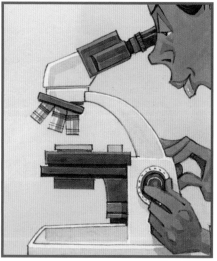

GERMS (OR MICROBES) ARE TINY, and they are everywhere. They get into your body and attack it from inside. Most germs are viruses or bacteria.

VIRUSES are very small: about 100,000 could squeeze into a line just one millimetre long. Flu and covid-19 are both diseases caused by viruses.

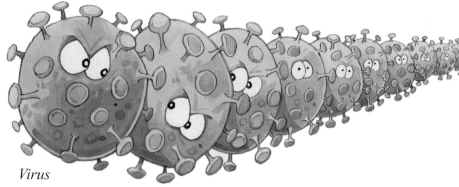

Virus

Just catching my breath – back soon!

Asthma makes breathing hard, but is easily controlled with medicine. You can't catch it!

Handy hint

Stop germs spreading! Cover your nose and mouth with a tissue when sneezing or coughing. Then bin it!

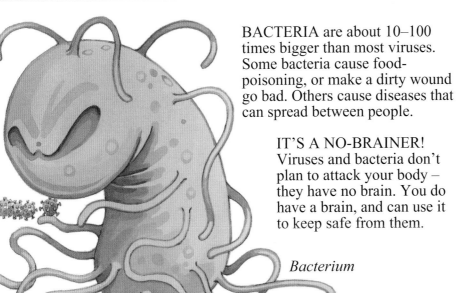

BACTERIA are about 10–100 times bigger than most viruses. Some bacteria cause food-poisoning, or make a dirty wound go bad. Others cause diseases that can spread between people.

IT'S A NO-BRAINER! Viruses and bacteria don't plan to attack your body – they have no brain. You do have a brain, and can use it to keep safe from them.

Bacterium

I, virus

Many diseases that cause epidemics or pandemics are caused by viruses. A virus is on the border between living and non-living things. It doesn't need food or air and can't move around on its own. All it can do is reproduce (make copies of itself). It's not an organism as it doesn't have even one cell. Many scientists call it a 'biological entity'. There are more viruses on Earth than all other biological entities put together. They are everywhere – in the air, the soil, the sea and our bodies.

We're taking over!

The life of a virus

WE VIRUSES are just strands of genetic material in a protein envelope. We can't move, eat or breathe – it's a pretty boring existence.

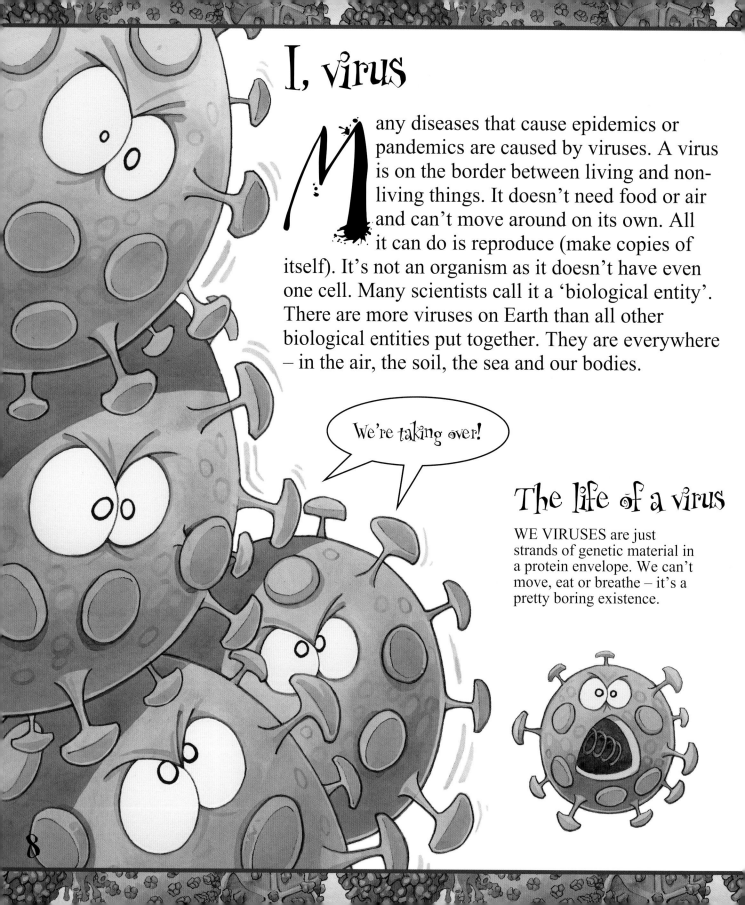

Rogues' gallery

Meet some of the deadliest viruses. We're all different but we can all be really nasty. You wouldn't want to meet any of us on a dark night!

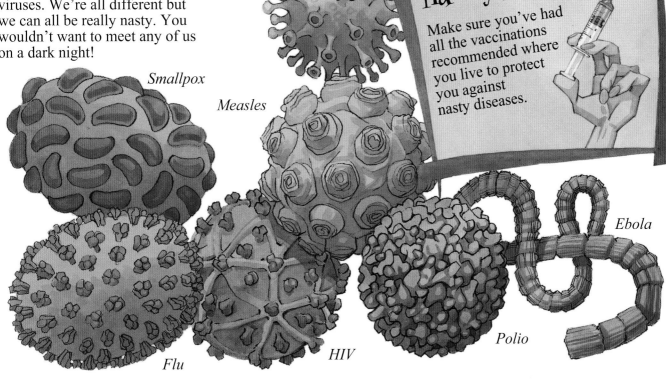

Covid-19

Smallpox

Measles

Flu

HIV

Polio

Ebola

Handy hint

Make sure you've had all the vaccinations recommended where you live to protect you against nasty diseases.

STEP 1: I'll latch onto one of your cells. Then either your cell will drag me inside, or I'll inject my genetic material into your cell. I'll get in somehow!

STEP 2: Inside, I'll take over the cell's resources and mechanisms to make copies of my bits. Your own cell will assemble them into ready-to-go viruses.

STEP 3: The new virus particles will burst out, destroying your cell, or bud from its surface. Then off they go to infect more cells!

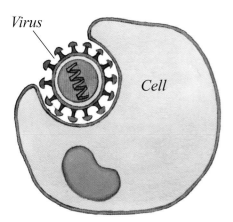

Virus

Cell

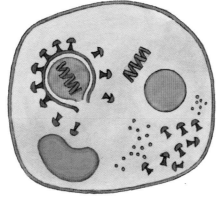

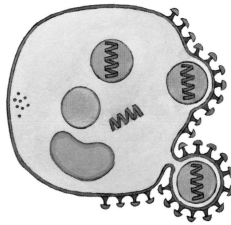

Not the first time

The 1500s

About 10,000 years ago, people began to settle and farm land. As they started living close to each other and to domesticated animals, diseases began to pass between them. People lived even more closely packed in cities, and epidemics began. Moving around for trade, war or exploration brought the chance to spread diseases even more widely – and a new threat of pandemics.

Pandemics make a lot of people ill and sometimes kill many of them. But that's not all. By disrupting societies, they can lead to war, famine (shortages of food) and political unrest. They often change the course of history.

You need me more than I need you.

430 BC

A PANDEMIC that swept across Libya, Ethiopia, Egypt and Greece in 430 BC killed up to two thirds of the population. In Greece, sick Athenian soldiers lost a war against the Spartans.

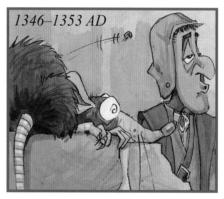

1346–1353 AD

THE BLACK DEATH of 1346–53 was the worst pandemic. Spread by fleas that live on rats, it killed most people who caught it – and it kept coming back for centuries.

PEASANT POWER. So many people died in the Black Death that farms lay unfarmed and people starved. A shortage of workers led to social unrest as peasants could demand better pay.

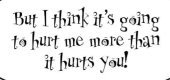

But I think it's going to hurt me more than it hurts you!

Plague kept coming back after the Black Death. In the 1500s, plague doctors tried useless and often painful 'remedies' on their poor patients.

Handy hint

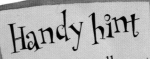

If you're unwell with an infectious disease, stay home until you're better – don't spread it!

AIRBORNE. Past pandemics spread slowly as people didn't move as far or fast as they do now. The Black Death spread over years. 1918-flu took only months to spread, carried by ship. Today, a disease can spread around the world in days or hours, carried by people flying between continents.

It's just a touch of flu.

1492 AD onwards

1918–1920

We don't do that sort of thing over here.

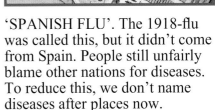

THE NEW WORLD. Europeans invading and colonizing the Americas took diseases that were new to local people. Smallpox, measles and flu killed up to 90 per cent of the population.

IN 1918–20, a massive flu pandemic spread across the world. It came at the end of the First World War when soldiers were moving around and people were weakened by years of hardship.

'SPANISH FLU'. The 1918-flu was called this, but it didn't come from Spain. People still unfairly blame other nations for diseases. To reduce this, we don't name diseases after places now.

11

Where do diseases come from?

Viruses and bacteria evolve over time. As they copy themselves, there's sometimes a mistake in the copy – a mutation – changing it a bit. Most mutations make no difference to how the virus affects us, but they can make it more or less harmful. Flu viruses mutate quickly. You need a new flu jab each year to protect you as flu viruses change so much from year to year.

Viruses can also grab bits of genetic material from another virus – even from one that usually infects a pig or chicken. If there are two viruses in a cell at once, they can mix and make a new virus. The 1918-flu came from a human flu and a bird flu mixing.

In the Middle Ages plucked chickens were rubbed on boils to treat the plague.

Keep your boils to yourself!

Pangolin

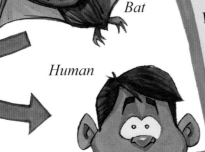

Bat

Human

Handy hint

Don't believe everything you read! Check the science, and don't pass on wacky ideas – they can be dangerous.

ANIMAL ORIGINS? The virus that caused covid-19 started in bats, and may have passed to humans through pangolins illegally sold for meat and medicine.

This is worse than the plague!

◀ TYPHUS. Diseases that are around at a low level can flare into an epidemic or pandemic if there is a war or famine. Often, in past wars, more soldiers died of typhus than of battle injuries.

▶ SUPERNATURAL. In the past, people often thought diseases were caused by angry gods. They prayed, made offerings, whipped themselves or built churches to try to stop an epidemic.

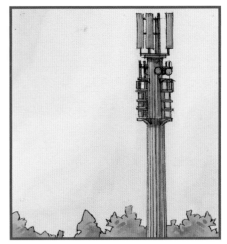

GERM WARFARE. Armies have used deadly diseases as weapons. Invading Mongols catapulted plague bodies into the city of Caffa, and Europeans spread smallpox to native Americans.

SCARY SCIENCE? Scientists can make or change viruses, and grow bacteria. Some people worry that a disease could be released accidentally, or that terrorists could even use a disease as a weapon.

5G. Some people even believed covid-19 was caused by 5G mobile phone signals. This is completely impossible. But when people are frightened, they will believe almost anything – especially if it seems to offer an easy answer.

It's catching!

For a disease to cause a pandemic it must spread between people readily. It spreads most easily if people can pass it on before they feel ill. People who feel ill stay at home, away from others.

To spread, a pathogen (germ that causes disease) shouldn't kill people too quickly, so they have a chance to pass it on. Dead people don't breathe out germs, so if the victim dies, the pathogen is stuck and can't move on. And it's best not to kill everyone – mild cases are much better for spreading a disease.

A pathogen's wish-list – great for germs, not so good for you!

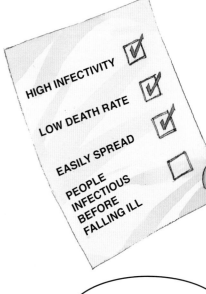

HIGH INFECTIVITY ✓

LOW DEATH RATE ✓

EASILY SPREAD ✓

PEOPLE INFECTIOUS BEFORE FALLING ILL ☐

Water's a bit dodgy today...

DROPLETS. Disease can pass between people in different ways. Flu and covid-19 are carried in droplets that people breathe out. Coughs and sneezes are great at spreading diseases!

BODY FLUIDS. Ebola is carried in body fluids such as blood. Cholera is passed on through drinking water that is polluted with excrement (poo) from infected people. Yuck!

R number

The reproduction number, R, is the average number of people each infected person infects. If R is 1 or lower, the disease won't spread well. Pandemic diseases have a high R value. For flu, it's around 2; for measles, it's 12–18.

R value = 3; first person (black) infects three others (red)

14

Handy hint

In a pandemic, don't go to parties and events, or hang out in crowded places.

CIRCUS

FOULA. Sometimes it's not the disease but the people who die out. When smallpox came to the Scottish Island of Foula in 1720, all but six of the inhabitants died.

EBOLA is scary: it kills 70% of people who catch it. But it won't make a pandemic as people aren't infectious until they're very ill. Health workers use protective gear to treat them.

People who recover often can't be reinfected. When many people that an infected person meets are immune, spread of the disease slows. A vaccination programme speeds this up, giving immunity to people who haven't had the disease.

Previously infected people (pink) each infect three more (red); recovered people are safe (green)

15

Stop the spread

When cases of a threatening disease appear, governments and health services try to prevent an epidemic or pandemic. If they can't, they try to limit its impact – how far and how fast it spreads, how many people get ill, and how many people die.

A major pandemic affects even people who don't fall ill. Patients with other medical conditions can't always get the treatments they need if hospitals are busy, and workers lose their jobs and livelihoods if businesses close.

WHO? A dangerous outbreak is reported to the World Health Organization (WHO). Researchers create tests so that they can tell when people have the disease.

When it's time to stop

TRAVEL RESTRICTIONS stop people carrying the disease elsewhere. People might need to prove they are healthy to travel. Whole cities are sealed off.

LOCKDOWN. People are told to stay in their homes, stay off work or school and only go out for essential trips, such as to buy food or medicines.

QUARANTINED. People with the disease, or who have been with someone who has it, are quarantined. If the disease can't spread, it dies out.

I don't mind staying inside!

Handy hint

During a pandemic, clean anything you bring into the house from shops or other people.

It's people like him that started this!

Flattening the infection curve helps hospitals cope.

High infection rate over a short period of time.

Infection rate spread out more slowly over a longer period of time.

FLATTEN THE CURVE. Countries try to slow the spread of a disease so that their health service is not overwhelmed. The same number of people might catch the disease, but it's easier to deal with them spread out.

THE BLAME GAME. In the past, people often blamed those from unpopular social groups for causing or spreading disease. We now know diseases are spread in the same way by people of all groups and that no one is to blame.

Deep breaths!

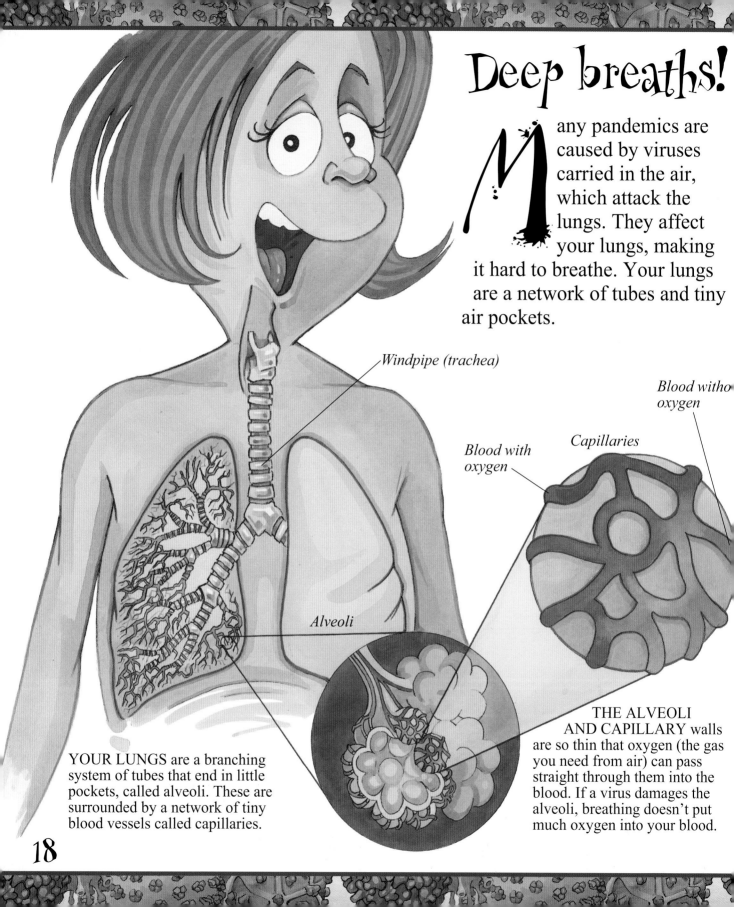

Many pandemics are caused by viruses carried in the air, which attack the lungs. They affect your lungs, making it hard to breathe. Your lungs are a network of tubes and tiny air pockets.

Windpipe (trachea)

Blood without oxygen

Capillaries

Blood with oxygen

Alveoli

YOUR LUNGS are a branching system of tubes that end in little pockets, called alveoli. These are surrounded by a network of tiny blood vessels called capillaries.

THE ALVEOLI AND CAPILLARY walls are so thin that oxygen (the gas you need from air) can pass straight through them into the blood. If a virus damages the alveoli, breathing doesn't put much oxygen into your blood.

A virus can make its home deep in your lungs, at the junction between the outside world's air and the inside world of your body. It can cause chaos, killing cells and blocking your lungs so that you struggle for breath, cough and splutter.

Handy hint

A face covering helps to protect people from disease. It traps some of the water droplets that carry germs.

A TOUCHY SUBJECT. You might breathe in a virus, or get it into your nose, mouth or eyes from your fingers. Lots of illnesses get into your body in this way.

VIRAL PARTICLES that get inside take over cells and reproduce. The new particles attack nearby cells, travelling further down your airways right into the alveoli.

INFECTED CELLS can't get on with their normal activity. They are damaged and eventually destroyed by the virus breaking out.

DEAD CELLS build up in the lungs as nasty gunk. Oxygen can't get to the blood. This makes you cough to get rid of the gunk.

19

Fighting back

Your body has an immune system to fight against infections. It recognises anything that is not part of you and attacks it. It makes special cells to fight the invaders, and remembers how to make the cells so it can produce its attack force quickly and efficiently.

A virus has chemicals on its surface called antigens. You make antibodies to fit each new antigen. The antibodies allow special immune cells to latch onto the antigens and destroy the virus. Once your body starts to make the right antibodies, it should be only a matter of time before the virus is defeated and you're healthy again.

Immune cells

Virus

Immune system cells recognise and destroy your body's enemies.

Handy hint

Taking exercise, eating healthy food and getting enough sleep will keep you fighting fit!

SYMPTOMS. When you're ill, it's often your own body that makes you feel bad. Chemicals it makes to fight illness can give you a fever, a headache, or aching muscles.

◀ RECOVERY. Usually, your body and the virus battle it out over a few days and you win. You get better as the number of virus particles in your body falls.

◀ OVERLOAD. Sometimes, the immune system is too keen and goes overboard. It can flood the body with chemicals that can harm the body's organs. People with an extreme immune system response need extra help to get better.

▶ OVERWORKED. Sometimes, the immune system is overwhelmed with too many viral particles. These people need extra help, too.

◀ MEMORY CELLS. Once you've had a disease, special memory cells remember how to make the antibodies for it. If you meet the same disease again, your body can fast-track making the right antibodies.

I'm sure I recognise you!

▶ AGE. Often, older people or people with other health problems are most vulnerable. Young, fit people with a good immune system are usually well protected.

You won't get me, virus!

21

Calling in reinforcements

In a pandemic, many people fall ill in a short space of time. Not everyone will need to go to hospital, as they won't all be very unwell. That's lucky, as there's not space in hospital for everyone who falls ill. Only those who are most unwell go to hospital, but even they can quickly fill hospital wards. Not catching it is the best option!

We don't yet have proper cures for diseases like flu and covid-19. Instead, people can take medicines to help them feel better as their immune system helps them to fight the disease. If they are very ill, doctors can help their body to get through the infection.

SOOTHING THE PAIN. Treating symptoms makes a sick person feel better while their body fights an infection. Creams can make you itch less when you have chickenpox, but they don't get rid of the virus.

BREATHTAKING. Diseases like flu, covid-19 or SARS make it difficult to breathe. In hospital, doctors can give patients extra oxygen to keep their body going whilst it fights the infection.

ANTIBIOTICS. Some diseases can be treated. If the Black Death happened now, we could use antibiotics to treat people and help them get better. Antibiotics kill the bacteria that cause an infection, but they don't work against a virus.

Handy hint
If you fall ill, stay indoors, keep warm, rest, drink lots of water and take medicine if you need to.

Ventilator

Air flows in → *Tube goes from mouth into throat*

Air flows out

VENTILATOR. A person who is very ill needs more help. Doctors might put them on a machine called a ventilator to take over their breathing. The ventilator's air tube goes into their throat.

SCIENTISTS research diseases all the time: there's lots of work still to do finding treatments and vaccines. Maybe you will be a medical scientist and make an important breakthrough?

Be prepared

This vaccine is years in the making!

When a new infection emerges, researchers rush to develop tests and vaccines. Vaccines work by showing the immune system what the antigen is like so that it can make antibodies. If a vaccinated person later encounters the disease, their body knows how to fight it, so they don't get ill. It takes a long time to work out how to make a vaccine and test it to check it works and is safe. It's not a quick fix for a new disease.

The two tests

Swab

THE FIRST TEST researchers try to develop tests to see if someone has the disease. It might need a throat or nose swab or a blood sample, for instance, to check for the antigen of the disease in blood or mucus.

THE SECOND TEST is for the antibody to fight the infection. If a person has antibodies in their blood, they're protected against the disease.

Handy hint

An antibody test can show if you've had a disease. You might not need a vaccine if you have.

A VACCINE gives the body a practice run with a form of the germ that can't cause the illness. It shows the body how to make the antibodies.

We know this one. Let's get it!

HUMAN TRIALS. A vaccine is first tested just with cells in a laboratory. If it works, it's then tested on small and then larger groups of people to make sure it works and is safe.

A LONG WAIT? A working vaccine is great. But there are nearly eight billion people in the world. It takes a long time to make and distribute eight billion shots of vaccine! This means that the world might have to live with a new disease for a long time before it can be conquered.

VACCINE ▷

Look after yourself – and others

During a pandemic, we all need to look after our health carefully. There's lots you can do to help protect yourself and other people. With many diseases, some people get the disease but show little or no sign of illness – they are asymptomatic. This happened during the covid-19 pandemic. People can also pass on a disease before they develop symptoms themselves, so even if you feel well you might be infectious.

ASYMPTOMATIC. Someone with no symptoms might still be able to spread it to other people, who could become very ill. They won't be asymptomatic just because the person they caught it from was.

Of course a cake is essential shopping!

STOP

COVID·19

Everyday activities like shopping are quite different in a pandemic – but we can adapt to do them safely.

WATCH THE CLOCK. Germs can survive for a while on surfaces, so it's important to keep your hands clean. Wash them thoroughly for at least 20 seconds with soap and hot water or clean them with hand sanitizer. This stops you moving germs from things you touch to your mouth, nose or eyes.

Handy hint

Be prepared! Make a 'pandemic pack' with disposable gloves, masks and hand sanitizer.

HEROES WEAR MASKS. If you have to go out, wear a protective mask. You're less likely to infect other people when wearing a mask, or to get infected yourself.

KEEP YOUR DISTANCE – at least one metre (ideally two metres) from other people. Many of the droplets you each breathe out will fall downwards in the gap between you.

USE A TISSUE to cover your face if you cough or sneeze. If you don't have a tissue, use the inside of your elbow.

MIND THE GAP. If you have to go somewhere crowded or use public transport, stay as far away as you can from people who don't live with you. You can still talk across the gap!

DON'T TOUCH! Avoid touching other people, or objects others have touched. If you have to touch things, wear disposable plastic gloves. Think about all the things people touch: the buttons on pedestrian crossings, door handles, light switches – there are lots!

OK for now

If there is a pandemic while you are reading this book, it will end one day (and more quickly if everyone acts sensibly). If there isn't, there will be another pandemic one day, so it's worth knowing how to deal with it. There was a gap of 100 years between 1918-flu and the covid-19 pandemic, but such a long time between bad pandemics is rare. With each one, we learn more about how best to protect people. With luck, we learn from mistakes and will do better next time. In a pandemic, we need to work together to protect everyone.

'HERD IMMUNITY' emerges when it's hard for a disease to spread because most people are immune. If an infected person can't pass the disease on, the pandemic dies down. It happens when many people have already had the disease or have been vaccinated.

DISEASES CHANGE as bacteria and viruses evolve. Reports of pandemics more than 1,000 years ago can't always be matched to modern diseases. Some diseases seem to have gone for good or changed a lot.

28   *Immune* 👤   *Infected* 👤

We need to take care for a long time after a pandemic eases – it can come back.

Needs to be two metres all round!

Handy hint

Even when there's no pandemic, washing your hands will help you avoid infections. Wash before eating and after going to the loo.

I wouldn't...

HIDDEN AWAY. Some diseases hide for long periods in animals. Bubonic plague affects marmots, gerbils (not pet gerbils!) and other rodents but is now rare in humans. But it can affect people who eat or handle infected animals.

SMALLPOX. Our greatest medical triumph was against smallpox. After a worldwide programme of vaccinating everyone at risk, the disease was wiped out by 1980. A couple of samples survive in research laboratories, but no one catches smallpox any more. We won!

We won!

Top plagues you wouldn't want to get!

1: The Black Death (bubonic plague), 1346–53

The most terrifying pandemic of all time spread from Asia to Europe and North Africa. It made people really, really ill and a lot of them really, really dead. Up to half the population of affected areas died, 75–200 million people. It had three forms. The most common, bubonic plague, was spread by fleas. Victims developed painful, large, black buboes (boils), which led to the name 'Black Death'. Plague returned for hundreds of years.

2: 'Spanish' flu, 1918–20

Although it was 'just' flu, around two in every hundred people died – up to 50 or even 100 million people worldwide from a population of two billion. Young, healthy people were hit hardest as their immune systems responded over-enthusiastically. It was wrongly named 'Spanish' flu because Spain was the only country that reported it fully. Other countries, busy fighting the First World War, hid news of infection which they felt would encourage their enemies.

4: Cholera, 1817–1824

The first of several cholera pandemics began in India and spread to Indonesia, China, Japan, Europe, Russia and the Middle East, killing millions. Cholera is spread through infected drinking water or food. Sufferers die from dehydration caused by extreme diarrhoea and vomiting.

3: Smallpox, measles, flu, bubonic plague, from 1492

Europeans carried many diseases to the Americas during their invasion and colonization. These infected local people who had never encountered them before and had no immunity to them. Up to 90 per cent of the inhabitants of some areas died – around 56 million people.

5: HIV/AIDS, 1981 onwards

Starting in chimpanzees, HIV/AIDS became a pandemic in 1981, beginning in Africa and then North America. AIDS destroys a person's immune system, so they die of other infections which they can't fight. So far, 35 million people have died of HIV/AIDS and 38 million live with it. It can now be controlled by medicines, but not cured.

Pandemic and epidemic timeline

165-180 AD

The Antonine plague, an unidentified disease that might have been measles or smallpox, killed five million people in Europe.

1520 AD

Newly introduced diseases including smallpox, measles and flu killed 56 million indigenous North and South Americans.

1346-1353 AD

The Black Death – bubonic plague and its septicaemic and pneumonic variants – ravaged Asia, Europe and North Africa, killing 75–200 million people. Smaller waves of this pandemic returned until the 1800s.

541-542 AD

In the Plague of Justinian, bubonic plague caused 30–50 million deaths. It kept coming back until 750 AD.

17th and 18th centuries

The Great Plagues of Europe were waves of bubonic plague and its variants that caused three million deaths.

1918-20

A strain of deadly flu starting in the USA caused a worldwide catastrophe, killing 25–100 million people.

1981 (ongoing)

HIV/AIDS; worldwide, 25–35 million deaths.

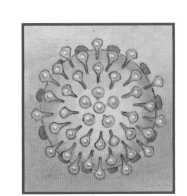

2019- (ongoing)

The covid-19 pandemic began in Wuhan, China, in 2019 and spread around the world. It causes breathing difficulties, but can damage many organs besides the lungs. The disease and its long-term effects are not yet properly understood. It caused more than one million deaths in its first year.

1855-1960s

The third plague pandemic swept the world, doing its worst in India and China. Alexandre Yersin identified the bacterium that causes plague in 1894, and it began to be treated with antibiotics in the 1900s.

You wouldn't want to be... treated for plague!

Modern treatments for pandemic diseases include antibiotics (if it's bacterial), anti-viral medicines (if it's viral) and oxygen to help breathing. In the past, when people didn't understand what caused diseases or how they spread, treatments were often wild and not-so-wonderful.

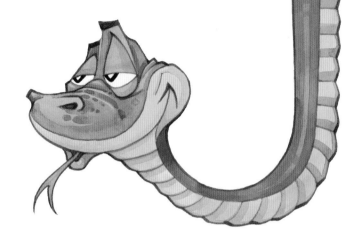

If you had plague, you might like to try holding a plucked chicken against your boils. (The chicken might not like it so much.)

Or you could drink the magical-sounding 'Venice treacle', or theriac, which had lots of ingredients, including roasted snake. It had to mature for 12 years, which made it expensive – and not a quick fix in a pandemic.

You could try a plague medicine made from powdered unicorn horn (if you could find a unicorn).

Burning strong-smelling wood and herbs was a fairly easy thing to do.

Some doctors thought people with plague had too much blood. That was easily solved with a jar of blood-sucking leeches.

You don't like leeches? A knife is just as good. Unfortunately, neither method worked.

Just a little scratch...

Pandemics and where they start

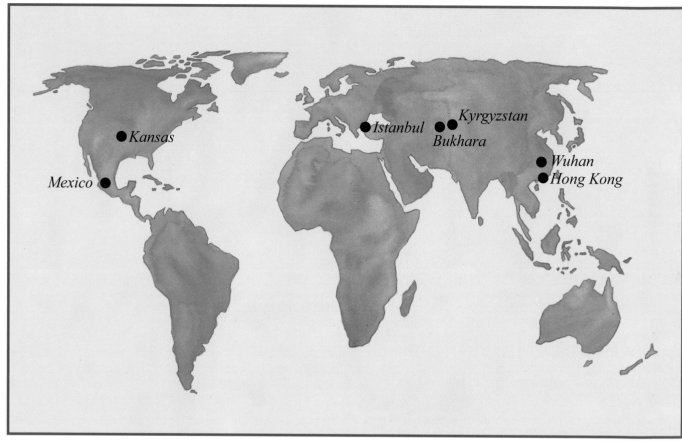

Kyrgyzstan: Possible start of the Black Death, 1346–53.

Kansas, USA: Likely start of 1918-flu.

Wuhan, China: Start of covid-19, 2019.

Istanbul, Turkey: Start of Plague of Justinian, 541–2 AD.

Mexico: Start of swine flu, 2009–10.

Bukhara: Source of Russian flu, 1889–90, the first pandemic spread by modern transport (rail).

Mexico City (Tenochtitlan): Cortés introduces smallpox to South America, 1521.

Hong Kong: Start of Hong Kong flu, 1968–70.

Glossary

Antibiotic A medicine to kill bacteria.

Antibody A cell produced by the body to fight germs.

Antigen A chemical on the surface of a virus or bacterium that triggers the immune system to get to work.

Anti-viral A medicine to fight a virus.

Asymptomatic With no symptoms (physical effects) of a disease.

Bacteria (singular **bacterium**) A type of living organism with a single cell.

Black Death The pandemic of bubonic plague and related forms of the disease that spread through Asia, Europe and part of Africa in 1346-50.

Bubonic plague A deadly bacterial disease usually started by a bite from an infected flea. The infection travels through the body's lymph system.

Cell A self-contained unit of a living organism.

Dehydration Losing water.

Ebola A viral disease that causes fever and bleeding inside and outside the body.

Epidemic A large number of cases of a disease in a short period of time.

Evolve To change in form or behaviour as a result of genetic changes between generations of an organism.

Famine An extreme shortage of food, causing people to starve.

Fever A state in which the body temperature rises, causing illness.

Genetic material Chemicals which carry a 'recipe' for an organism.

Germ A microbe or virus that causes disease.

Immune Not able to catch a disease.

Immune system The body's protective system that fights infections.

Glossary continued

Infectious Capable of producing or passing on an infection.

Marmot A giant ground squirrel.

Measles A very infectious viral disease that causes fever and a rash.

Microbe An organism so small it's visible only with a microscope.

Mucus A slimy liquid that is produced by the body.

Mutation A mistake made when a cell or organism reproduces, producing a copy a bit different from its parent.

Pandemic A very widespread epidemic.

Pathogen A microbe or virus that causes a disease.

Pneumonic plague A version of plague that is spread by droplets in the breath.

Protein A type of chemical important in building the bodies of organisms.

Quarantine A period of isolation.

Reproduction number/R value The rate at which an infection spreads, shown as how many extra people each infected person infects.

SARS A viral respiratory disease.

Septicaemic plague A version of plague that is carried in the blood.

Smallpox A deadly viral disease that causes a fever and rash of blisters.

Symptom A physical sign of illness.

Typhus A group of bacterial diseases that cause fever and a rash.

Vaccination, vaccine Using a safe version of a disease to prompt the body to make antibodies for future protection.

Virus A tiny biological entity that can cause disease.

WHO (World Health Organization) A worldwide body to protect health.

Index